365 INSPIRATIONS

nature

&

beauty

365 INSPIRATIONS

nature

&

beauty

DUNCAN BAIRD PUBLISHERS

LONDON

365 Inspirations: Nature & Beauty

General Editor: Emma Maule

Distributed in the USA and Canada by Sterling Publishing Co., Inc.
387 Park Avenue South, New York, NY 10016-8810

This edition first published in the UK and USA in 2007 by
Duncan Baird Publishers Ltd
Sixth Floor, Castle House, 75–76 Wells Street, London W1T 3QH

Assistant Editor: Kirty Topiwala
Managing Designer: Clare Thorpe
Designer: Louise Leffler
Picture research: Susannah Stone

Library of Congress Cataloging-in-Publication Data Available
10 9 8 7 6 5 4 3 2 1
ISBN-13: 978-1-84483-492-1   ISBN-10: 1-84483-492-1

Typeset in Gill Sans and Charme
Color reproduction by Scanhouse, Malaysia
Printed by Imago, Thailand

For information about custom editions, special sales, premium and corporate
purchases, please contact Sterling Special Sales Department at 800-805-5489
or specialsales@sterlingpub.com.

NOTES

Abbreviations used throughout this book:

CE Common Era (the equivalent of AD)

BCE Before the Common Era (the equivalent of BC)

b. born, d. died

Contents

Foreword

Nature lives in our surroundings, in ourselves and in the connections between the two.

The Taoists saw unobstructed rivers and streams as a model for harmonious living, while the Romantics, many centuries later, found in the wilderness an important corrective to the formalized distortions that had infiltrated society. Even the least soulful among us is likely to find in nature an antidote to something – whether duplicity, or repression, or commercialism, or just plain stress.

The idea of nature as cosmos does not contradict the less spiritual concept of nature as beautiful landscape, with all its teeming fauna. At one end of the spectrum, landscape satisfies the aesthetic sense; at the other end, we see the intricate workings of the watch and start to speculate on the watchmaker. Somewhere in the middle, "delightful" shifts to "awesome" and the notion of the Sublime takes root, with overtones of humanity's littleness against a global or cosmic backdrop.

The phenomena that lie visibly beyond us can acquire extra significance when transformed by human imagination and skill. This is the opposite side of beauty's coin – works of art, literature, music, dance, design, architecture.

Between the points of the equilateral triangle – self, nature and art – complex energies playfully, movingly and profoundly interact. It is no accident that the "mystery of creation" is an ambiguous phrase. In their overtones of mood and meaning, the words succinctly encapsulate the theme of this gathering of quotations from different regions, ages and traditions. Travel inwardly and relish the experience.

Earth, sky and stars

The cosmos

1 *All and nothing*

I am the dust in the sunlight, I am the ball of the sun.
I am the mist of morning, the breath of evening.
I am the spark in the stone, the gleam of gold in the metal.
The rose and the nightingale drunk with its fragrance.
I am the chain of being, the circle of the spheres,
The scale of creation, the rise and the fall.
I am what is and is not ...
I am the soul in all.

Jalil al-Din Rumi (1207–1273), Persia

2 The universal body

We and the cosmos are one. The cosmos is a vast body, of which we are still parts. The sun is a great heart whose tremors run through our smallest veins. The moon is a great gleaming nerve-centre from which we quiver forever. Who knows the power that Saturn has over us or Venus? But it is a vital power, rippling exquisitely through us all the time ...

Now all this is literally true, as men knew in the great past and as they will know again.

D.H. Lawrence (1885–1930), England

3 *Perfection*

We shall affirm that the cosmos, more than anything else, resembles
most closely that living Creature of which all other living creatures,
severally or genetically, are portion; a living creature which is fairest
of all and in many ways most perfect.

Plato (c.429–c.347 BCE), *Greece*

4 Web of being

Constantly think of the Universe as one living
creature, embracing one being and one soul;
how all is absorbed into the one consciousness
of this living creature; how it compasses all things
with a single purpose, and how all things work
together to cause all that comes to pass, and
their wonderful web and texture.

Marcus Aurelius (121–180), Rome

5 In harmony

All things are parts of one single system, which
is called Nature; the individual life is good when
it is in harmony with Nature.

Zeno of Citium (300–260 BCE), Cyprus

6 Unconsidered

Nothing puzzles me more than time and space; and yet nothing troubles me less, as I never think about them.

Charles Lamb (1775–1834), England

7 *A haiku*

The world? Moonlit
drops shaken
from the crane's bill.

Dogen (1200–1253), Japan

8 Neverending circles

Nature is an infinite sphere of which the centre is everywhere and the circumference nowhere.

Blaise Pascal (1623–1662), France

9 A question of scale

I don't pretend to understand the Universe – it's a great deal bigger than I am.

Thomas Carlyle (1795–1881), Scotland/England

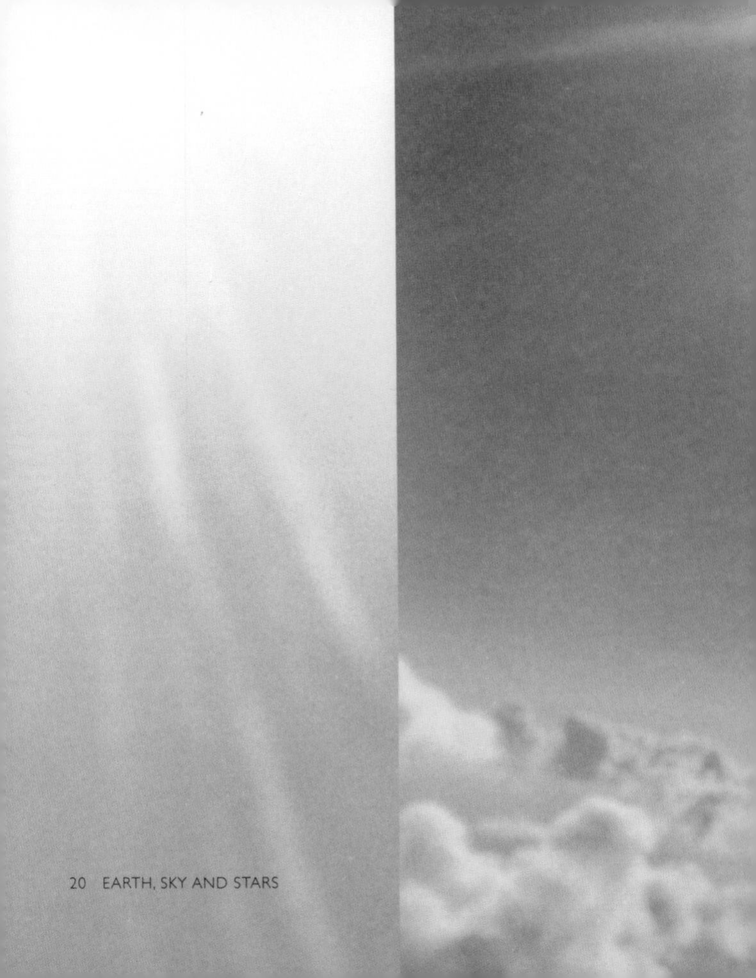

10 Chorus of stars

Everything lives, moves, everything corresponds; the magnetic rays, emanating either from myself or from others, cross the limitless chain of created things unimpeded; it is a transparent network that covers the world, and its slender threads communicate themselves by degrees to the planets and stars. Captive now upon earth, I commune with the chorus of the stars who share in my joys and sorrows.

Gérard de Nerval (1808–1855), France

Our planet

11 Fire cycle

The world, an entity out of everything, was created by neither
gods nor men, but was, is and will be eternally living fire,
regularly becoming ignited and regularly becoming extinguished.

Heraclitus (c. 535 – c. 475 BCE), Greece

12 Stardust

Unknowingly, we plough the dust of stars, blown about us by the
wind, and drink the universe in a glass of rain.

Ihab Hassan (b. 1925), Egypt/USA

13 *Cherish it well*

And God saw everything that He had made, and found it
very good.
And He said: "This is a beautiful world that I have given you.
Take good care of it; do not ruin it."
It is said that before the world was created, the Holy One kept
creating worlds and destroying them.
Finally He created this one, and was satisfied.
He said to Adam: "This is the last world I shall make. I place
it in your hands: hold it in trust."

Jewish parable

14 The World

It burns in the void,
Nothing upholds it.
Still it travels.

Burning it travels,
The void upholds it
Still it is nothing.

Travelling the void
Upheld by burning
Nothing is still.

Nothing it travels
A burning void
Upheld by stillness.

Kathleen Raine (1908–2003), England

15 Bigger picture

What's the use of a fine house if you haven't got a tolerable planet to put it on?

Henry David Thoreau (1817–1862), USA

16 Lost in space

The man who doesn't know what the universe is doesn't know where he lives.

Marcus Aurelius (121–180), Rome

17 This green earth

I am in love with this green earth; the face
of town and country; the unspeakable rural
solitudes and the sweet security of the streets.

Charles Lamb (1775–1834), England

18 A close family

Breathe to me, sheep in the meadow. Sun and moon,
my father and my father's brother, kiss me on the brow
with your light. My sister, earth, holds me up to be kissed.
Sun and moon, I smile at you both and spread my arms in
affection and lay myself down at full length for the earth
to know I love it too and am never to be separated from
it. In no way shall death part us.

David Ignatow (1914–1997), USA

19 *Planetary hygiene*

When you've finished getting yourself ready in the morning, then it is time to get your planet ready, just so, with the greatest care.

Antoine de Saint-Exupéry (1900–1944), France

Weather

20 Unpredictable

Climate is what we expect, weather is what we get.

Mark Twain (1835–1910), USA

21 Letting things happen

Too often man handles life as he does the bad weather,
He whiles away the time as he waits for it to stop.

Alfred Polgar (1873–1955), Switzerland/Austria

22 Barometer

A cloudy day or a little sunshine have as great an influence on many constitutions as the most recent blessings or misfortunes.

Joseph Addison (1672–1719), England

23 Dazzling beams

Give me the splendid silent sun with all his beams full-dazzling.

Walt Whitman (1819–1892), USA

24 April Rain Song

Let the rain kiss you,
Let the rain beat upon your head with silver liquid drops,
Let the rain sing you a lullaby,
The rain makes still pools on the sidewalk,
The rain makes running pools in the gutter,
The rain plays a little sleep song on our roof at night,
And I love the rain.

Langston Hughes (1902–1967), USA

25 Unappreciated

Many a man curses the rain that falls upon his head, and knows not that it brings abundance to drive away the hunger.

Basile Giambattista (1575–1632), Italy

26 Yielding ways

The weathercock on the church spire,
though made of iron, would soon
be broken by the storm-wind if it
did not understand the noble art
of turning to every wind.

Heinrich Heine (1797–1856), Germany

27 No such thing

Sunshine is delicious, rain is refreshing,
wind braces us up, snow is exhilarating;
there is really no such thing as bad weather,
only different kinds of good weather.

John Ruskin (1819–1900), England

The seasons

28 Zen gardening

Sitting quietly, doing nothing, spring comes,
and the grass grows by itself.

Buddhist proverb

29 Spring prayer

Everywhere is the green of new growth ...
We notice the bright green atop the dark green on the pine, the fir,
the hemlock, the spruce, the cedar.
The alder is already in leaf.
The locust is late as always.
Everywhere and always the song of birds ... bees raiding the orchard,
raccoon prowling at nightfall, the earthworm tunneling the garden,
chickens and rabbits pecking and nibbling, the goats tugging to reach
new delights ... all are the ubiquitous energies of life.

O Lord,
May we today be touched by grace, fascinated and moved by this
your creation, energized by the power of new growth at work in
your world.
May we move beyond viewing this life only through a frame, but
   touch it and be touched by it,
   know it and be known by it,
   love it and be loved by it.

From the Chinook Psalter

30 High spirits

A little Madness in the Spring
Is wholesome even for the King.

Emily Dickinson (1830 – 1886), USA

31 Communion

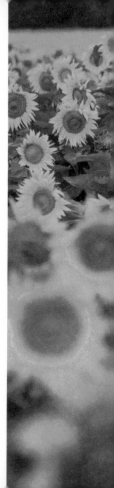

I walk without flinching through the burning cathedral of the summer. My bank of wild grass is majestic and full of music. It is a fire that solitude presses against my lips.

Violette Leduc (1907–1972), France

32 Intoxication

Summer is the time when one sheds one's tensions with one's clothes, and the right kind of day is jeweled balm for the battered spirit. A few of those days and you can become drunk with the belief that all's right with the world.

Ada Louise Huxtable (b.1921), USA

33 Music to my ears

Summer afternoon – Summer afternoon ...
the two most beautiful words in the English language.

Henry James (1843–1916), USA/England

34 Sound advice

It will not always be summer:
build barns.

Hesiod (c.700 BCE), Greece

35 Time of joy

In summer, the song sings itself.

William Carlos Williams (1883–1963), USA

36 Last smile

Autumn … the year's last,
loveliest smile.

John H. Bryant (1807–1833), USA

37 *Flowers and fruits*

Youth is like spring, an over-praised season more
remarkable for biting winds than genial breezes.
Autumn is the mellower season, and what we lose
in flowers we more than gain in fruits.

Samuel Butler (1835–1902), England/New Zealand

38 Bridal voyage

Delicious autumn! My very soul is wedded to it,
and if I were a bird I would fly about the earth
seeking the successive autumns.

George Eliot (1819–1880), England

39 Delayed message

Antisthenes says that in a certain faraway land the
cold is so intense that words freeze as soon as they
are uttered, and only after some time they thaw and
become audible, so that words spoken in winter go
unheard until the next summer.

Plutarch (c.45–125 CE), Greece

40 Winter sun

What fire could ever equal the sunshine of a winter's day, when the meadow mice come out by the wall-sides, and the chickadee lisps in the defiles of the wood? The warmth comes directly from the sun, and is not radiated from the earth, as in summer; and when we feel his beams on our backs as we are treading some snowy dell, we are grateful as for a special kindness, and bless the sun which has followed us into that by-place.

Henry David Thoreau (1817–1862), USA

41 *Golden moments*

Winter, a lingering season, is a time to gather golden moments, embark upon a sentimental journey and enjoy every idle hour.

Jane Young (b.1947), England

42 Sowing

Let us love winter, for it is the spring of genius.

Pietro Aretino (1492–1556), Italy

43 Compassion

One kind word can warm three winter months.

Japanese proverb

Miracles of nature

44 *Opposite*

Miracles are not contrary to nature,
but only contrary to what we know
about nature.

St Augustine of Hippo (354–430),
North Africa

45 *Flower power*

If no one had ever seen a flower,
even a dandelion would be the most
startling event in the world.

Helen Keller (1880–1968), USA

46 Cry of the universe

We are the miracle of force and matter making itself over into imagination and will. Incredible. The Life Force experimenting with forms. You for one. Me for another. The Universe has shouted itself alive. We are one of the shouts.

Ray Bradbury (b.1920), USA

47 *Beneath it all*

Nothing is rich but the inexhaustible wealth of nature.
She shows us only surfaces, but she is a million fathoms deep.

Ralph Waldo Emerson (1803–1882), USA

48 *Watchful eye*

Observe the marvels as they happen around you. Don't claim them.
Feel the beauty moving through and be silent.

Jalil al-Din Rumi (1207–1273), Persia

49 His handiwork

Nature is the art of God.

Sir Thomas Browne (1605–1682), England

50 *Minor masterpiece*

I believe a leaf of grass is no less than the journey-work of the stars.

Walt Whitman (1819–1892), USA

51 Sparks and shadows

What is life? It is the flash of a firefly in the night.
It is the breath of a buffalo in the wintertime.
It is the little shadow which runs across the grass
and loses itself in the sunset.

Chief Crowfoot (c.1830–1890), his last words, Canada

52 In awe

To me every hour of the light and dark is a miracle.
Every cubic inch of space is a miracle.

Walt Whitman (1819–1892), USA

53 Open portal

If we could see the miracle of a single flower clearly, our whole life would change.

The Buddha (c.563–c.483BCE), India

54 Comedy

When you realize how perfect everything is you will tilt your head back and laugh at the sky.

The Buddha (c.563–c.483BCE), India

God's design

55 Letting us be

I believe in Spinoza's God who reveals himself in the orderly harmony of what exists, not in a God who concerns himself with fates and actions of human beings.

Albert Einstein (1879–1955), Germany/USA

56 Divine scripture

Never lose an opportunity of seeing anything beautiful,
for beauty is God's handwriting.

Ralph Waldo Emerson (1803–1882), USA

57 Incarnation

The highest revelation is that God is in every man.

Ralph Waldo Emerson (1803–1882), USA

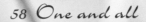

58 One and all

All things come out of the One
and the One out of all things.

Heraclitus (c.535–c.475 BCE), Greece

59 The motivator

God is the great mysterious motivator of what we call nature, and it has often been said by philosophers that nature is the will of God. And I prefer to say that nature is the only body of God that we shall ever see.

Frank Lloyd Wright (1867–1959), USA

60 Allspice

God is day and night, winter and summer, war and peace, fullness and hunger; he changes the way fire does when mixed with spices and is named according to each spice.

Heraclitus (c.535 – c.475 BCE), Greece

61 Thoughts on design

I cannot imagine how the clockwork of the universe can exist without a clockmaker.

Voltaire (1694–1778), France

62 Just so

If God had wanted me otherwise,
He would have created me otherwise.

*Johann Wolfgang von Goethe (1749–1832),
Germany*

The heavens

63 An equal rising

The sun rose on the flawless brimming sea into a sky
all brazen — all one brightening for gods immortal and
for mortal men on ploughlands kind with grain.

Homer (8th century BCE), from The Odyssey, *Greece*

64 Blithe star

The sun, with all those planets revolving around it and
dependent on it, can still ripen a bunch of grapes as if
it had nothing else in the universe to do.

Galileo Galilei (1564–1642), Italy

65 Full moon

The growing and dying of the moon reminds us of
our ignorance, which comes and goes; but when the
moon is full, it is as if the eternal light of the Great
Spirit were upon the whole world.

Black Elk (1863–1950), USA

66 Celestial food

The sky is the daily bread of the eyes.

Ralph Waldo Emerson (1803–1882), USA

67 The Starlight Night

Look at the stars! look, look up at the skies!
    O look at all the fire-folk sitting in the air!
    The bright boroughs, the circle-citadels there!
Down in dim woods the diamond delves! the elves'-eyes!
The grey lawns cold where gold, where quickgold lies!
    Wind-beat whitebeam! airy abeles set on a flare!
    Flake-doves sent floating forth at a farmyard scare!
Ah well! it is all a purchase, all is a prize.
Buy then! bid then! – What! – Prayer, patience, alms, vows.
Look, look: a May-mess, like on orchard boughs!
    Look! March-bloom, like on mealed-with-yellow sallows!
These are indeed the barn; withindoors house
The shocks. This piece-bright paling shuts the spouse
    Christ home, Christ and his mother and all his hallows.

Gerard Manley Hopkins (1844–1889), England
(abeles: white poplar trees)

68 Misty river

My companion and I were alone with the stars: the misty river of the Milky Way flowing across the sky, the patterns of the constellations standing out bright and clear, a blazing planet low on the horizon. It occurred to me that if this were a sight that could be seen only once in a century, this little headland would be thronged with spectators. But it can be seen many scores of nights in any year, and so the lights burned in the cottages and the inhabitants probably gave not a thought to the beauty overhead; and because they could see it almost any night, perhaps they never will.

Rachel Carson (1907–1964), USA

69 Footloose

Mortal as I am, I know that I am born for a day. But when I follow at my pleasure the serried multitude of the stars in their circular course, my feet no longer touch the earth.

Ptolemy (c.90 – c.168CE), Egypt

70 Bedtime ritual

It seemed to be a necessary ritual that he should prepare himself for sleep by meditating under the solemnity of the night sky ... a mysterious transaction between the infinity of the soul and the infinity of the universe.

Victor Hugo (1802–1885), France

Men and women

The body

Humanity

Life-spans

Grace and movement

Adornment

The body

71 Open book

Love's mysteries in souls do grow,
But yet the body is his book.

John Donne (1572–1631), England

72 Wise blood

The body is a big sagacity, a plurality with one sense,
a war and a peace, a flock and a shepherd.

Friedrich Nietzsche (1844–1900), Germany

73 Praise be

Know ye not that your body is the temple of the Holy Ghost which is in you, which ye have of God, and ye are not your own? For ye are bought with a price: therefore glorify God in your body and in your spirit, which are God's.

1 Corinthians 6:19

74 Flesh and blood

The body that is sown is perishable, it is raised imperishable ...
If there is a natural body, there is also a spiritual body ...
I declare to you, brothers, that flesh and blood cannot inherit the
kingdom of God, nor does the perishable inherit the imperishable.

I Corinthians *15:35–50*

75 All there is

Make the most of yourself,
for that is all there is of you.

Ralph Waldo Emerson (1803–1882), USA

76 Expressive

The soul that can speak through the
eyes can also kiss with a gaze.

Gustavo Adolfo Bécquer (1836–1870), Spain

77 Sacred ground

Here in this body are the sacred rivers: here are the sun and moon, as well as all the pilgrimage places. I have not encountered another temple as blissful as my own body.

Mahasiddha Saraha (late 8th century), India

78 *In a glance*

An eye can threaten like a loaded and leveled gun, or it can insult like hissing or kicking; or, in its altered mood, by beams of kindness, it can make the heart dance for joy ...

One of the most wonderful things in nature is a glance of the eye; it transcends speech; it is the bodily symbol of identity.

Ralph Waldo Emerson (1803–1882), USA

79 *Why beauty?*

If eyes were made for seeing, then beauty is its own excuse for being.

Ralph Waldo Emerson (1803–1882), USA

80 Quiet secrets

The face is the mirror of the mind, and eyes without speaking confess the secrets of the heart.

St Jerome (c.340–420), Israel

81 Insight

You must look into people, as well as at them.

Lord Chesterfield (1694–1773), England

Humanity

82 Made to measure

For thou hast made him a little lower than the angels,
and hast crowned him with glory and honour.

Psalms *8:5*

83 Best and worst

Man, when perfected, is the best of animals, but, when
separated from law and justice, he is the worst of all.

Aristotle (384–322 BCE), Greece

84 Strange creature

What a chimera, then, is man! What a novelty, what a monster, what a chaos, what a subject of contradiction, what a prodigy! A judge of all things, feeble worm of the earth, depositary of the truth, cloaca of uncertainty and error, the glory and the shame of the universe!

Blaise Pascal (1623–1662), France

85 Empathy

Could a greater miracle take place than for us
to look through each other's eyes for an instant?

Henry David Thoreau (1817–1862), USA

86 Beauty spot

Beauty is the mark God sets upon virtue.

Ralph Waldo Emerson (1803–1882), USA

87 Helping hand

There is a loftier ambition than merely to stand high in the world. It is to stoop down and lift mankind a little higher.

Henry van Dyke (1852–1933), USA

88 A lovely virtue

Humanity is never so beautiful as when praying for forgiveness, or else forgiving another.

Jean Paul Richter (1763–1825), Germany

89 *Aspirations*

There are those who will say that the liberation
of humanity, the freedom of man and mind is
nothing but a dream. They are right. It is the
American Dream.

Archibald MacLeish (1892–1982), USA

Life-spans

90 An olive, ripening

Mark how fleeting and paltry is the estate of man
– yesterday in embryo, tomorrow a mummy or ashes.
So for the hair's breadth of time assigned to thee, live
rationally and part with life cheerfully, as drops the
ripe olive, extolling the season that bore it and the
tree that matured it.

Marcus Aurelius (121–180), Rome

91 Fearless

Even death is not to be feared by one who has lived wisely.

The Buddha (c.563–c.483 BCE), *India*

92 Master of fate

If we have been pleased with life, we should not be displeased with death, since it comes from the hand of the same master.

Michelangelo (1475–1564), Italy

93 Ancient and modern

To be ignorant of what happened before you were born is to be ever
a child. For what is man's lifetime unless the memory of past events
is woven with those of earlier times?

Cicero (c.106–43 BCE), *Rome*

94 Already there

The Scholar: Whither goes the soul when the body dies?
The Master: There is no necessity for it to go anywhere.

Jacob Böhme (1575–1624), Germany

95 Behind and beyond

The span of life allotted to man is very short; the World
in which he lives is very wide; time extends far behind
and far beyond.

From the Atharva Veda (c.2nd century BCE), India

96 Gleam of time

One life – a little gleam of Time
between two Eternities.

Thomas Carlyle (1795–1881), Scotland/England

97 Eternal bond

We are the living links in a life force
that moves and plays around and
through us, binding the deepest soils
with the farthest stars.

Alan Chadwick (1909–1980), England/USA

Grace and movement

98 Dancing deity

I would only believe in a god who knew how to dance.

Friedrich Nietzsche (1844–1900), Germany

99 Celestial skills

It is no doubt possible to fly – but first you must know how to dance like an angel.

Friedrich Nietzsche (1844–1900), Germany

100 Endless wave

When you do dance, I wish you
A wave o'the sea, that you might ever do
Nothing but that, move still, still so,
And own no other function.

William Shakespeare (1564–1616),
from The Winter's Tale, *England*

101 Flowing arcs

In life, as in art, the beautiful moves in curves.

Edward Bulwer-Lytton (1803–1873), England

102 Playtime

Play is the exultation of the possible.

Martin Buber (1878–1965), Austria

103 Youthful instincts

How inimitably graceful children are in general – before they learn to dance.

Samuel Taylor Coleridge (1772–1834), England

104 Poetry in motion

The dance is a poem of which each movement is a world.

Mata Hari (1876–1917), Netherlands/France

105 Weather wise

Movement never lies. It is a barometer telling the state of the soul's weather.

Martha Graham (1894–1991), USA

Adornment

106 Inner beauty

I would rather be adorned by beauty of character than jewels. Jewels are the gift of fortune, while character comes from within.

Plautus (254–184 BCE), Rome

107 Simply done

The most beautiful subjects? The simplest and the least clad.

Anatole France (1844–1924), France

108 Behind a veil

A beauty masked, like the sun in eclipse, gathers together more gazers than if it shined out.

William Wycherley (1640–1716), England

109 High price

A crown, if it hurt us, is hardly worth wearing.

Philip James Bailey (1816–1902), England

110 Unaffected

Most works are beautiful without ornament.

Walt Whitman (1819–1892), USA

111 Effortless

Outward simplicity befits ordinary men, like a garment made to measure for them; but it serves as an adornment to those who have filled their lives with great deeds: they might be compared to some beauty carelessly dressed and thereby all the more attractive.

Jean de La Bruyère (1645–1696), France

112 Integral whole

True ornament is not a matter of prettifying externals. It is organic with the structure it adorns, whether a person, a building, or a park.

Frank Lloyd Wright (1867–1959), USA

The living world

Natural beauty

113 *Pied Beauty*

Glory be to God for dappled things –
　For skies of couple-colour as a brinded cow;
　　　For rose-moles all in stipple upon trout that swim;
Fresh-firecoal chestnut-falls; finches' wings;
　Landscape plotted and pieced – fold, fallow, and plough;
　　　And all trades, their gear and tackle and trim.
All things counter, original, spare, strange;
　Whatever is fickle, freckled (who knows how?)
　　　With swift, slow; sweet, sour; adazzle, dim;
He fathers-forth whose beauty is past change:
　　　Praise him.

Gerard Manley Hopkins (1844–1889), England

114 Natural cure

The best remedy for those who are afraid, lonely or unhappy is to go outside, somewhere where they can be quiet, alone with the heavens, nature and God. Because only then does one feel that all is as it should be and that God wishes to see people happy, amidst the simple beauty of nature.

Anne Frank (1929–1945), Netherlands

115 Self-contained

Whatever is in any way beautiful has its source
of beauty in itself and is complete in itself.

Marcus Aurelius (121–180), Rome

116 Back to basics

It is a wholesome and necessary thing for us to
turn again to the earth and in the contemplation
of her beauties to know of wonder and humility.

Juan Formoza (1890–1921), Brazil

117 *Microscopic*

Nature will bear the closest inspection. She invites us to lay our eye level with her smallest leaf and take an insect view of its plain.

Henry David Thoreau (1817–1862), USA

The land

118 Persistence

Enough shovels of earth – a mountain.
Enough pails of water – a river.

Chinese proverb

119 *Skyscape*

For me, a landscape does not exist in its own right, since its appearance changes at every moment; but the surrounding atmosphere brings it to life – the light and the air which vary continually. For me, it is only the surrounding atmosphere which gives subjects their true value.

Claude Monet (1840–1926), France

120 *Picnic*

Nothing helps scenery like ham and eggs.

Mark Twain (1835–1910), USA

121 *Rustic rhythm*

There is nothing like walking to get the feel of a country.
A fine landscape is like a piece of music; it must be taken
at the right tempo. Even a bicycle goes too fast.

Paul Scott Mowrer (1887–1971), USA

122 Ownership

You forget that the fruits belong to all and that the land belongs to no one.

Jean-Jacques Rousseau (1712–1778), Switzerland/France

123 Simple rule

One does not sell the land people walk on.

Crazy Horse (1849–1877), USA

124 In chains

It is preoccupation with
possession, more than anything
else, that prevents men from
living freely and nobly.

Bertrand Russell (1872–1970), England/USA

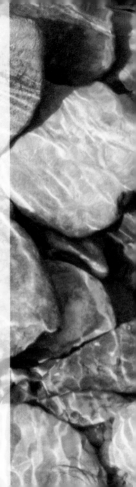

Earth and stone

125 Private fancy

The pebble in the brook secretly thinks
itself a precious stone.

Japanese proverb

126 Trying at least

Better a diamond with a flaw than
a pebble without.

Confucius (551–479 BCE), China

127 Song of the Earth Spirit

It is lovely indeed, it is lovely indeed.
I, I am the spirit within the earth.
The feet of the earth are my feet;
The legs of the earth are my legs.
The strength of the earth is my strength;
The thoughts of the earth are my thoughts;
The voice of the earth is my voice.
The feather of the earth is my feather;
All that belongs to the earth belongs to me;
All that surrounds the earth surrounds me.
I, I am the sacred works of the earth.
It is lovely indeed, it is lovely indeed.

From a Navajo legend

128 *Primal pulse*

Healthy feet can hear the very heart of the Holy Earth.

Chief Sitting Bull (1831–1890), USA

129 Healing power

Man and man's earth are unexhausted and undiscovered.
Wake and listen! Verily, the earth shall yet be a source of
recovery. Remain faithful to the earth, with the power of
your virtue. Let your gift-giving love and your knowledge
serve the meaning of the earth.

Friedrich Nietzsche (1844–1900), Germany

130 Real mystery

We know more about the movement of celestial bodies
than about the soil underfoot.

Leonardo da Vinci (1452–1519), Italy

131 To the Mother

O Mother Earth, You are the earthly source of all
existence. The fruits which You bear are the source of life
for the Earth peoples. You are always watching over Your
fruits as does a mother. May the steps which we take in
life upon You be sacred and not weak.

Oglala Sioux prayer

132 *Motherboard*

Land, then, is not merely soil: it is a fountain
of energy flowing through a circuit of soils,
plants, and animals.

Aldo Leopold (1887–1948), USA

Animals

133 Ethical measure

The greatness of a nation and its moral progress
can be judged by the way its animals are treated.

Mahatma Gandhi (1869–1948), India

134 *Our humble brethren*

Not to hurt our humble brethren (the animals) is our first duty to them, but to stop there is not enough. We have a higher mission — to be of service to them whenever they require it ...

   If you have men who will exclude any of God's creatures from the shelter of compassion and pity, you will have men who will deal likewise with their fellow men.

St Francis of Assisi (1182–1228), Italy

135 *So it follows*

Compassion for animals is intimately connected with goodness of character; and it may be confidently asserted that he who is cruel to animals cannot be a good man.

Arthur Schopenhauer (1788–1860), Germany

136 Criterion

When a man has pity on all living creatures, only then is he noble.

The Buddha (c.563 – c.483 BCE), India

137 Respect for all

Respect the old and cherish the young. Even insects, grass and trees you must not hurt.

Ko Hung (c.284 – 343), China

138 Two sides of a coin

The fact that man knows right from wrong proves his intellectual superiority to the other creatures; but the fact that he can do wrong proves his moral inferiority to any creatures that cannot.

Mark Twain (1835–1910), USA

139 Comparison of species

I have been studying the traits and dispositions of the "lower animals" (so called) and contrasting them with the traits and dispositions of man. I find the result humiliating to me.

Mark Twain (1835–1910), USA

140 Wild wisdom

Animals, in their generation, are wiser than the sons of men; but their wisdom is confined to a few particulars and lies in a very narrow compass.

Joseph Addison (1672–1719), England

141 Easy departure

Animals have these advantages over man: they never hear the clock strike, they die without any idea of death, they have no theologians to instruct them, their last moments are not disturbed by unwelcome and unpleasant ceremonies, their funerals cost them nothing and no one starts lawsuits over their wills.

Voltaire (1694–1778), France

142 Good friends

Animals are such agreeable friends — they ask
no questions, they pass no criticisms.

George Eliot (1819–1880), England

143 Company of fools

The greatest pleasure of a dog is that you may make
a fool of yourself with him, and not only will he not
scold you, but he will make a fool of himself too.

Samuel Butler (1835–1902), England/New Zealand

144 Feline friend

It is quite something to gain the affection of a cat. He is a philosophical animal, tenacious of his own habits, fond of order and neatness, and disinclined to extravagant sentiment. He will be your friend, if he finds you worthy of friendship, but not your slave.

Théophile Gautier (1811–1872), France

145 Living plaything

When I play with my cat, who knows if I am not a pastime for her more than she is to me?

Michel de Montaigne (1533–1592), France

146 *Fine example*

The elephant, not only the largest but the most intelligent of animals, provides us with an excellent example. It is faithful and tenderly loving to the female of its choice, mating only every third year and then for no more than five days and so secretly as never to be seen, until, on the sixth day, it appears and goes at once to wash its whole body in the river, unwilling to return to the herd until thus purified. Such good and modest habits are an example to husband and wife.

St Francis de Sales (1567–1622), France/Switzerland

147 Workforce

The bee is more honoured than other animals, not because she labours, but because she labours for others.

St John Chrysostom (c.347–c.407), Turkey

148 Gentle souls

Cows are amongst the gentlest of breathing creatures;
none show more passionate tenderness to their young
when deprived of them; and, in short, I am not ashamed
to profess a deep love for these quiet creatures.

Thomas de Quincey (1785–1859), England

149 Look up and see

When thou seest an eagle, thou seest a portion of
genius; lift up thy head.

William Blake (1757–1827), England

Plants and flowers

150 Simply happy

Look at the trees, look at the birds, look at the clouds, look at the stars ... and if you have eyes you will be able to see that the whole existence is joyful. Everything is simply happy. Trees are happy for no reason; they are not going to become prime ministers or presidents and they are not going to become rich and they will never have any bank balance. Look at the flowers – happy for no reason. It is simply unbelievable how happy flowers are.

Osho (1931–1990), India/USA

151 Bright blooms of hope

Stars of earth, these golden flowers; emblems of our own
great resurrection; emblems of the bright and better land.

Henry Wadsworth Longfellow (1807–1882), USA

152 The sweetest things

Flowers are the sweetest things God ever made,
and forgot to put a soul into.

Henry Ward Beecher (1813–1887), USA

153 *Strange sowing*

He who plants thorns must never expect to gather roses.

Arabian proverb

154 *How little we know*

They tell us that plants are not like man immortal,
but are perishable – soul-less. I think that is something
that we know exactly nothing about.

John Muir (1838–1914), Scotland/USA

155 Future perfect

We have much to hope from the flowers.

Sir Arthur Conan Doyle (1859–1930), Scotland/England

156 Chuckling

The Earth laughs in flowers.

Ralph Waldo Emerson (1803–1882), USA

157 Quiet chimes

The temple bell stops
but I still hear the sound
coming out of the flowers.

Basho (1644–1694), Japan

158 Gentle ministrations

Science, or para-science, tells us that geraniums bloom better if they are spoken to. But a kind word every now and then is really quite enough. Too much attention, like too much feeding and weeding and hoeing, inhibits and embarrasses them.

Sybil Frances Grey (1867–1943), England

Forests and woods

159 A tree's longing

That tree whose leaves are trembling:
Is yearning for something.
That tree so lovely to see acts as if it wants to flower:
It is yearning for something.

Diego Hurtado de Mendoza (1503–1575), Spain

160 Clothed in green

The forest is the poor person's fur coat.

Estonian proverb

161 Endless effort

Trees are the earth's endless effort
to speak to the listening heaven.

Rabindranath Tagore (1861–1941), India

162 Tree teachings

Study the teachings
of the pine tree,
the bamboo
and the plum blossom.
The pine is evergreen,
firmly rooted
and venerable.
The bamboo is strong,
resilient,
unbreakable.
The plum blossom is hardy,
fragrant
and elegant.

Morihei Ueshiba (1883–1969), Japan

163 Serene majesty

There is a serene and settled majesty to woodland scenery
that enters into the soul and delights and elevates it, and fills
it with noble inclinations.

Washington Irving (1783–1859), USA

164 Dante's dark wood

Midway upon the journey of our life
    I found myself within a forest dark,
    For the straightforward pathway had been lost.
Ah me! how hard a thing it is to say
    What was this forest savage, rough, and stern,
    Which in the very thought renews the fear.

Dante Alighieri (1256–1321), Italy

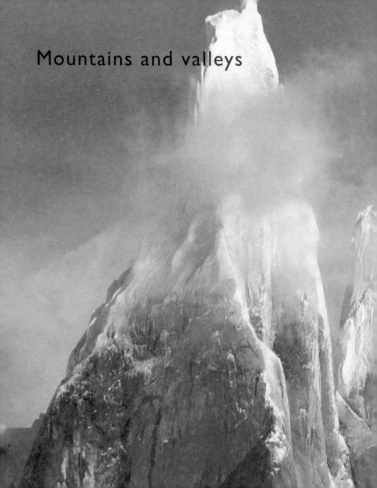

Mountains and valleys

165 Timeless treasures

Mountains are earth's undecaying monuments.

Nathaniel Hawthorne (1804–1864), USA

166 Alpha and omega

Mountains are the beginning and the end of all natural scenery.

John Ruskin (1819–1900), England

167 Giant leap

In the mountains, the shortest way is from peak to peak:
but for that you must have long legs.

Friedrich Nietzsche (1844–1900), Germany

168 Nightfall

The wind has settled, the blossoms have fallen;
Birds sing, the mountains grow dark –
This is the wonderful power of Buddhism.

Ryokan (1758–1831), Japan

169 Dividing lines

Mountains interposed
Make enemies of nations, who had else
Like kindred drops been mingled into one.

William Cowper (1731–1800), England

170 Keeping a distance

The heights charm us, but the steps do not; with the mountain in our view we love to walk the plains.

Johann Wolfgang von Goethe (1749–1832), Germany

171 Body and speech

The colour of the mountains is Buddha's body;
The sound of running water is his great speech.

Dogen (1200–1253), Japan

172 Muscle power

Mountains are to the rest of the body of the earth, what
violent muscular action is to the body of man. The muscles
and tendons of its anatomy are, in the mountain, brought
out with force and convulsive energy, full of expression,
passion and strength.

John Ruskin (1819–1900), England

173 Impossibility

Even God cannot make two mountains without a valley in between.

Gaelic proverb

174 On and on

Beyond the mountains there are mountains again.

Haitian proverb

175 Greetings

Climb the mountains and get their good tidings.

John Muir (1838–1914), Scotland/USA

The sea

176 Conclusion

Follow the river and you'll find the sea.

French proverb

177 Great waters

Thy way is in the sea, and thy path in the great waters, and thy footsteps are not known.

Psalms *77:19*

178 Wonderful water

There is no water in oxygen, no water in hydrogen: it comes bubbling fresh from the imagination of the living God, rushing from under the great white throne of the glacier. The very thought of it makes one gasp with an elemental joy no metaphysician can analyze. The water itself, that dances, and sings, and slakes the wonderful thirst – symbol and picture of that draught for which the woman of Samaria made her prayer to Jesus – this lovely thing itself, whose very wetness is a delight to every inch of the human body in its embrace – this live thing which, if I might, I would have running through my room, yea, babbling along my table – this water is its own self, its own truth, and is therein a truth of God.

George Macdonald (1824–1905), Scotland

179 High time

Whenever I find myself growing grim about the mouth; whenever it is a damp, drizzly November in my soul; whenever I find myself involuntarily pausing before coffin warehouses, and bringing up the rear of every funeral I meet; and especially whenever my hypos get such an upper hand of me, that it requires a strong moral principle to prevent me from deliberately stepping into the street, and methodically knocking people's hats off – then, I account it high time to get to sea as soon as I can.

Herman Melville (1819–1891), from Moby-Dick, *USA*

180 Ocean deep

The sea is everything. It covers seven tenths
of the terrestrial globe. Its breath is pure and
healthy. It is an immense desert, where man
is never lonely, for he feels life stirring on all
sides. The sea is only the embodiment of a
supernatural and wonderful existence.

Jules Verne (1828–1905), France

181 Speechless

Break, break, break,
On thy cold gray stones, O sea!
And I would that my tongue could utter
The thoughts that arise in me.

Alfred, Lord Tennyson (1809–1892), England

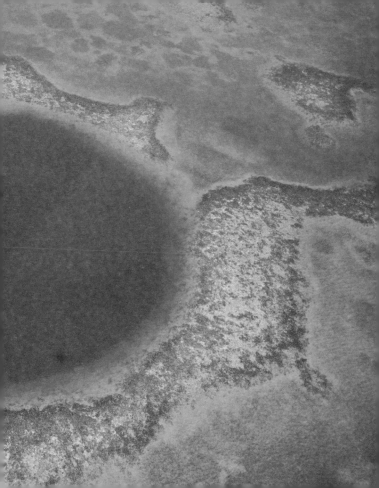

182 *Priceless rain*

The rain water enlivens all living beings of the earth both
movable (insects, animals, humans and so on), and immovable
(plants, trees and so on), and then returns to the ocean, its
value multiplied a millionfold.

Chanakya (350–275BCE), India

183 *The everflowing stream*

For all at last returns to the sea – to Oceanus, the ocean river,
like the everflowing stream of time, the beginning and the end.

Rachel Carson (1907–1964), USA

184 *Lessons in yearning*

If you want to build a ship, don't drum up people together to collect wood and don't assign them tasks and work, but rather teach them to long for the endless immensity of the sea.

Antoine de Saint-Exupéry (1900–1944), France

185 *Out of bounds*

Ocean: A body of water occupying about two-thirds of a world made for man – who has no gills.

Ambrose Bierce (1842–1914), USA

186 *Peace at last*

Finally out of reach –
No bondage, no dependency.
How calm the ocean,
Towering the void.

Zen Master Tessho's death poem (c.13th century), China

187 Mirror image

I have seen the sea when it is stormy and wild; when it is quiet and serene; when it is dark and moody. And in all its moods, I see myself.

Martin Buxbaum (1912–1991), USA

Streams, rivers and lakes

188 *Softly powerful*

Nothing in the world is more flexible and yielding than water.
Yet when it attacks the firm and the strong, none can withstand
it, because they have no way to change it. So the flexible
overcome the adamant, the yielding overcome the forceful.
Everyone knows this, but no one can do it.

Lao Tzu (c.604–c.531 BCE), *from the* Tao Te Ching, *China*

189 *All is flux*

In rivers, the water that you touch is the last of what has passed and the first of that which comes; so with present time.

Leonardo da Vinci (1452–1519), Italy

190 *Brotherly love*

The rivers are our brothers. They quench our thirst. They carry our canoes and feed our children. You must give to the rivers the kindness you would give to any brother.

Chief Seathl (1780–1866), USA

191 *Acknowledging the source*

When you drink from the stream, remember the spring.

Chinese proverb

192 My thoughts

The sound of the water says what I think.

Chuang Tzu (d. 275 BCE), China

193 Song of a thousand voices

The many-voiced song of the river echoed softly. Siddhartha looked into the river and saw many pictures in the flowing water. The river's voice was sorrowful. It sang with yearning and sadness, flowing towards its goal ... Siddhartha was now listening intently ... to this song of a thousand voices ... then the great song of a thousand voices consisted of one word: Om – Perfection ... From that hour Siddhartha ceased to fight against his destiny.

Hermann Hesse (1877–1962), from Siddhartha, *Germany/Switzerland*

194 *Lazy days*

The mark of a successful man is one that has spent an entire day on the bank of a river without feeling guilty about it.

Chinese proverb

195 Divine destiny

As different streams having different sources all mingle their waters in the sea, so different tendencies, various though they appear, crooked or straight, all lead to God.

Swami Vivekananda (1863–1902), India/USA

Spirits within

196 Careful whispers

Let us be silent, that we may hear the whispers of the gods.

Ralph Waldo Emerson (1803–1882), USA

197 Behind nature

I feel that God is behind every flower and every tree in the woods. He is behind every mountain rock and every foam-crested wave in the sea.

Thor Heyerdahl (1914–2002), Norway

198 *Ubiquitous*

Everywhere is God. The earth underneath us is his hand upholding us; the waters are in the hollow of it. Every spring-fountain of gladness about us is his making and his delight. He tends us and cares for us; he is close to us, breathing into our nostrils the breath of life, and breathing into our spirit thoughts that make us look up and recognize the love and care around us.

George Macdonald (1824–1905), Scotland

199 Lovely response

I asked the earth, I asked the sea and the deeps, among the living animals, the things that creep. I asked the winds that blow, I asked the heavens, the sun, the moon, the stars and all things that stand at the doors of my flesh ...

My question was the gaze I turned to them.

Their answer was their beauty.

St Augustine of Hippo (354–430), North Africa

200 Divine likeness

Beauty is God's reflection in the
swirling waters of the universe.

Lourdes Mallo (b.1930), Gran Canaria

201 Living planet

We might say that the earth has
the spirit of growth; that its flesh
is the soil.

Leonardo da Vinci (1452–1519), Italy

202 *All a-tremble*

There have been times when looking
up beneath the shelt'ring Trees,
I could invest every Leaf with Awe.

Samuel Taylor Coleridge (1772–1834), England

203 A sense sublime

For I have learned
To look on nature, not as in the hour
Of thoughtless youth, but hearing oftentimes
The still, sad music of humanity,
Nor harsh nor grating, though of ample power
To chasten and subdue. And I have felt
A presence that disturbs me with the joy
Of elevated thoughts; a sense sublime
Of something far more deeply interfused,
Whose dwelling is the light of setting suns,
And the round ocean, and the living air,
And the blue sky, and in the mind of man,
A motion and a spirit, that impels
All thinking things, all objects of all thought,
And rolls through all things.

William Wordsworth (1770–1850),
from Lines Composed a Few Miles above Tintern Abbey, *England*

Fertility

204 Under sail

A ship under sail and a big-bellied woman,
Are the handsomest two things that can be seen common.

Benjamin Franklin (1706–1790), USA

205 Earth wise

Consider what each soil will bear, and what each refuses.

Virgil (70–19BCE), Rome

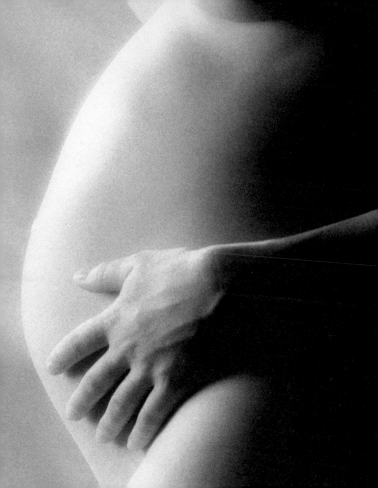

206 *Birthday*

A baby is God's opinion that life should go on.

Carl Sandburg (1878–1967), USA

207 Two smiles

A woman has two smiles that an angel might envy: the smile that accepts a lover before words are uttered, and the smile that lights on the first-born babe, and assures it of a mother's love.

Thomas C. Haliburton (1796–1865), Canada/England

208 Rule of heraldry

A simple maiden in her flower
Is worth a hundred coats-of-arms.

Alfred, Lord Tennyson (1809–1892), England

Living with nature

The simple life

Natural skills

Farming

Hunting and fishing

Gardening

Outward bound

Conservation

The simple life

209 *King of the pumpkin patch*

I would rather sit on a pumpkin and have it all to myself,
than be crowded on a velvet cushion.

Henry David Thoreau (1817–1862), USA

210 *Plainly content*

Manifest plainness,
Embrace simplicity,
Reduce selfishness,
Have few desires.

Lao Tzu (c.604–c.531 BCE), from the Tao Te Ching, *China*

211 In miniature

Living in retirement beyond the world,
Silently enjoying isolation,
I pull the rope of my door tighter
And stuff my window with roots and ferns.
My spirit is tuned to the spring-season:
At the fall of the year there is autumn in my heart.
Thus imitating cosmic changes,
My cottage becomes a universe.

Lu Yun (265–303), China

212 Clear sight

A life in harmony with nature, the love of truth and virtue,
will purge the eyes to understanding her text.

Ralph Waldo Emerson (1803–1882), USA

213 Free and easy

Live in the sunshine, swim the sea, drink the wild air …

Ralph Waldo Emerson (1803–1882), USA

214 Truly blessed

If you have a garden and a library,
you have everything you need.

Cicero (c.106–43 BCE), *Rome*

215 Happy days

With a few flowers in my garden,
half a dozen pictures and some
books, I live without envy.

Lope de Vega (1562–1635), Spain

216 *Bounteous gifts*

The day, water, sun, moon, night –
I do not have to purchase these things with money.

Plautus (254–184BCE), Rome

217 *Self-sufficient*

Maybe a person's time would be as well spent
raising food as raising money to buy food.

Frank A. Clark (b.1911), USA

218 *Modest pleasures*

To find the universal elements enough; to find the air and the water exhilarating; to be refreshed by a morning walk or an evening saunter ... to be thrilled by the stars at night; to be elated over a bird's nest or a wildflower in spring – these are some of the rewards of the simple life.

John Burroughs (1837–1921), USA

219 Sense and reason

That which we call Nature is therefore the power which
permeates and preserves the whole universe, and this power
is not devoid of sense and reason. Every being which is not
homogeneous and simple but complex and composite must
have in it some organizing principle. In man this organizing
principle is reason and in animals it is a power akin to reason,
and from this arises all purpose and desire.

Cicero (c.106–43BCE), *Rome*

Natural skills

220 Inside, outside

It is good to collect things; it is better to take walks.

Anatole France (1844–1924), France

221 Nature and nurture

Natural abilities are like natural plants; they need pruning by study.

Francis Bacon (1561–1626), England

222 *Mollycoddled*

There are two spiritual dangers in not owning a farm.
One is the danger of supposing that breakfast comes
from the grocery and the other that heat comes from
the furnace.

Aldo Leopold (1887–1948), USA

223 Chameleon

The art of life lies in a constant re-adjustment to our surroundings.

Kakuzo Okakura (1862–1913), Japan

224 Good practice

Only those who have to do simple things perfectly will acquire the skill to do difficult things easily.

Friedrich von Schiller (1759–1805), Germany

225 *Adverse conditions*

Skilful pilots gain their reputation from
storms and tempest.

Epicurus (341–270 BCE), Greece

226 *Seafaring*

'Tis skill, not strength, that governs a ship.

Thomas Fuller (1608–1661), England

Farming

227 Green fingers

Whoever could make two ears of corn or two blades of grass to grow upon a spot of ground where only one grew before, would deserve better of mankind, and do more essential service to his country than the whole race of politicians put together.

Jonathan Swift (1667–1745), from Gulliver's Travels, Ireland/England

228 On paper

Farming looks mighty easy when your plow is a pencil, and you're a thousand miles from the cornfield.

Dwight David Eisenhower (1890–1969), USA

229 Seedtime

Sowing is not as difficult as reaping.

Johann Wolfgang von Goethe (1749–1832), Germany

230 Botany

The greatest service which can be rendered to any country is to add a useful plant to its culture.

Thomas Jefferson (1743–1826), USA

231 Resurgence

Though you drive nature out with a pitchfork, she will still find her way back.

Horace (65–8 BCE), Rome

232 *Wholeness*

We must learn not to disassociate the airy flower from the earthy root, for the flower that is cut off from its root fades, and its seeds are barren, whereas the root, secure in mother earth, can produce flower after flower and bring their fruit to maturity.

The Kabbalah

233 *Country love*

Only he can understand what a farm is, what a country is, who shall have sacrificed part of himself to his farm or country, fought to save it, struggled to make it beautiful. Only then will the love of farm or country fill his heart.

Antoine de Saint-Exupéry (1900–1944), France

234 Taking root

You work here on the farm simply, without philosophizing; sometimes the work is hard and crowded with pettiness. But at times you feel a surge of cosmic exaltation, like the clear light of the heavens … And you, too, seem to be taking root in the soil which you are digging, to be nourished by the rays of the sun, to share life with the tiniest blade of grass, with each flower; living in nature's depths, you seem then to rise and grow into the vast expanse of the universe.

Aaron David Gordon (1856–1922), Israel

Hunting and fishing

235 In waiting

The patience of the hunter is always greater than that of the prey.

Traditional saying

236 Animal history

Until the lions have their historians, tales of the hunt shall always glorify the hunter.

African proverb

237 Fertile ocean

We must plant the sea and herd its animals, using the sea as farmers instead of hunters. That is what civilization is all about – farming replacing hunting.

Jacques Yves Cousteau (1910–1997), France

238 *Double standards*

When a man wantonly destroys
one of the works of man we call
him a vandal. When he destroys
one of the works of god we call
him a sportsman.

Joseph Wood Krutch (1893–1970), USA

239 Horse sense

Though I am an old horse, and have seen and heard a great deal, I never yet could make out why men are so fond of this sport; they often hurt themselves, often spoil good horses, and tear up the fields, and all for a hare, or a fox, or a stag, that they could get more easily some other way; but we are only horses, and don't know.

Anna Sewell (1820–1878), from Black Beauty, *England*

240 Happy fisherman

I say, as I thus sat, joying in my own happy condition and pitying this poor rich man that owned this and many other pleasant groves and meadows about me, I did thankfully remember what my Saviour said, that the meek possess the earth; or rather they enjoy what the others possess and enjoy not; for Anglers and meek quiet-spirited men are free from those high, those restless thoughts which corrode the sweets of life.

Izaak Walton (1593–1683), England

241 Born not made

Angling is somewhat like poetry: men are to be born so.

Izaak Walton (1593–1683), England

Gardening

242 Reason meets nature

When all is said and done, is there any more wonderful sight, any moment when man's reason is nearer to some sort of contact with the nature of the world than the sowing of seeds, the planting of cuttings, the transplanting of shrubs or the grafting of slips.

St Augustine of Hippo (354–430), North Africa

243 Spade work

It is a blessed sort of work, and if Eve had had a spade in Paradise and known what to do with it, we should not have had all that sad business of the apple.

Elizabeth von Arnim (1866–1941), England/Germany

244 Seeds of joy

He who plants a garden plants happiness.

Chinese proverb

245 Mind and soil

The garden is a ground plot for the mind.

Thomas Hill (late 16th century), England

246 *Sunday service*

Some keep the Sabbath going to Church,
I keep it staying at Home –
With a bobolink for a Chorister,
And an Orchard, for a Dome.

Emily Dickinson (1830–1886), USA
(bobolink: small New World blackbird)

247 Blessings

A garden is a delight to the eye
and a solace for the soul.

Saadi (c.1210–c.1290), Persia

248 Fellow feeling

He that plants trees, loves others
besides himself.

Thomas Fuller (1608–1661), England

249 Abundance

Earth is here so kind, that just tickle her with a hoe and she laughs with a harvest.

Douglas Jerrold (1803–1857), England

250 *Hill of beans*

I used to visit and revisit it a dozen times a day, and stand in deep contemplation over my vegetable progeny with a love that nobody could share or conceive of who had never taken part in the process of creation. It was one of the most bewitching sights in the world to observe a hill of beans thrusting aside the soil, or a rose of early peas just peeping forth sufficiently to trace a line of delicate green.

Nathaniel Hawthorne (1804–1864), USA

251 Perfect place

I think that if ever a mortal heard the voice of God it would be in a garden at the cool of the day.

Frank Frankfort Moore (1855–1931), England

252 Revelation

Show me your garden and I shall tell you what you are.

Alfred Austin (1835–1913), England

Outward bound

253 *Self-control*

It is not the mountain that we conquer but ourselves.

Sir Edmund Hillary (b.1919), New Zealand

254 *Perfect balance*

Walking is the great adventure, the first meditation, a
practice of heartiness and soul primary to humankind.
Walking is the exact balance between spirit and humility.

Gary Snyder (b.1930), USA

255 Journey back

I offer no description of my return route to Berbera, as it was a mere adventure of uncommon hardship.

Richard Francis Burton (1821–1890), England

256 Nature's instruments

Perhaps my adventures and a short description of a city hitherto unvisited by Europeans may not be unacceptable to a society which, though essentially scientific, does not withhold encouragement from the pioneer of discovery, reduced by hard necessity to use nature's instruments – his eyes and ears.

Richard Francis Burton (1821–1890), England

257 Heavenly canopy

How hard to realize that every camp of men or beasts has this glorious starry firmament for a roof! In such places standing alone on the mountain-top it is easy to realize that whatever special nests we make — leaves and moss like the marmots and birds, or tents or piled stone — we all dwell in a house of one room — the world with the firmament for its roof — and are sailing the celestial spaces without leaving any track.

John Muir (1838–1914), Scotland/USA

258 Pull of the waves

The fishermen know that the sea is dangerous and the storm terrible, but they have never found these dangers sufficient reason for remaining ashore.

Vincent van Gogh (1853–1890), Netherlands/France

259 Venture forth

Without adventure civilization is in full decay.

Alfred North Whitehead (1861–1947), England/USA

Conservation

260 *Fallow fields*

For six years you are to sow your fields and harvest the crops,
but during the seventh year let the land lie unploughed and
unused. Then the poor among your people may get food from
it, and the wild animals may eat what they leave. Do the same
with your vineyard and your olive grove.

Exodus 23:10–11

261 *Loving the land*

We abuse land because we regard it as a commodity belonging
to us. When we see land as a community to which we belong,
we may begin to use it with love and respect.

Aldo Leopold (1887–1948), USA

262 Posterity

We must strive to become good ancestors.

Ralph Nader (b.1934), USA

263 Keep it pure

Drop no dirt into the well that's given you water.

English proverb

264 Wondering why

People wonder why the streams
are bitter, when they themselves
have poisoned the fountain.

John Locke (1632–1704), England

265 *Nuts and bolts*

Progress, under whose feet the grass mourns and the
forest turns into paper from which newspaper plants
grow, has subordinated the purpose of life to the means
of subsistence and turned us into the nuts and bolts for
our tools.

Karl Kraus (1874–1936), Germany

266 *Against tyranny*

Modern man no longer regards Nature as being in any
sense divine and feels perfectly free to behave towards
her as an overwhelming conqueror and tyrant.

Aldous Huxley (1894–1963), England/USA

267 *Good investment*

The nation behaves well if it treats the natural resources
as assets which it must turn over to the next generation
increased, and not impaired, in value.

Theodore Roosevelt (1858–1919), USA

268 Caretakers

Both group effort and individual testimony flow from conviction as to the role of people on earth. In stewardship of the common heritage, a few simple beliefs recur: that all are indeed members of the same human family, that all share in responsibility for the others, that each is capable of responding directly to divine guidance. To seek to translate these into practical action with regard to soil or petroleum or the fish of the sea is not necessarily to do what is directly effective in changing society; it is to testify to a way that is harmonious with one's fellows and with a healthy earth.

Gilbert F. White (1911–2006), USA

269 Tomorrow's Children

Our planet is our mother, our father
and our soul —

a blue pearl in the vast black emptiness.

Unless we repair the damage we have done,
our soul will go on burying itself
deeper and deeper
into the vast black emptiness ...

and our unborn children will go on crying
for love
in their darkness.

Jeanne Deneuve (b.1930), France

Fruits of imagination

Created beauty

Art

Music

Literature

Architecture and design

Truth and insight

The beauty of numbers

Created beauty

270 On the trail

The pursuit of perfection, then, is the pursuit of sweetness and light.

Matthew Arnold (1822–1888), England

271 Faultless piece

Whoever thinks a faultless piece to see,
Thinks what ne'er was, nor is, nor e'er
shall be.

Alexander Pope (1688–1744), England

272 One name

The ideal has many names, and beauty is but one of them.

Ninon de Lenclos (1620–1705), France

273 Agreement

Reality does not conform to the ideal, but confirms it.

Gustave Flaubert (1821–1880), France

274 Condensed

What is art? Nature concentrated.

Honoré de Balzac (1799–1850), France

275 Sublime shadow

The true work of art is but a shadow of the divine perfection.

Michelangelo (1475–1564), Italy

276 The only way

It is through Art, and through Art only, that we can realize our perfection.

Oscar Wilde (1854–1900), England

277 When to stop

Perfection is achieved, not when there is nothing more to add, but when there is nothing left to take away.

Antoine de Saint-Exupéry (1900–1944), France

278 *Fruitfulness*

As the soul ... cannot be productive without cultivation,
so the mind without culture can never produce good fruit.

Seneca (c.4 BCE–c.65 CE), *Rome*

279 How we live

The human soul has still greater need of the ideal than of the real. It is by the real that we exist; it is by the ideal that we live.

Victor Hugo (1802–1885), France

280 Search engine

Art is not a study of positive reality, but a seeking after ideal truth.

George Sand (1804–1876), France

Art

281 The painter's challenge

A good painter has two main objects to paint,
man and the intention of his soul. The former is
easy, the latter hard as he has to represent it by
the attitude and movement of the limbs.

Leonardo da Vinci (1452–1519), Italy

282 Combined effort

Where the spirit does not work with the hand,
there is no art.

Leonardo da Vinci (1452–1519), Italy

283 Unending

Art is never finished, only abandoned.

Leonardo da Vinci (1452–1519), Italy

284 Extremes

Art is either plagiarism or revolution.

Paul Gauguin (1848–1903), France

285 *Mental battlefield*

Art will remain the most astonishing activity of mankind born out of struggle between wisdom and madness, between dream and reality in our mind.

Magdalena Abakanowicz (b.1930), Poland

286 *Against the grain*

Yes, the work comes out more beautiful from a material that resists the process, be that verse, marble, onyx or enamel.

Théophile Gautier (1811–1872), France

287 *Necessary sacrifice*

Art is a kind of innate drive that seizes a human being and makes him its instrument. To perform this difficult office it is sometimes necessary for him to sacrifice happiness and everything that makes life worth living for the ordinary human being.

Carl Jung (1875–1961), Switzerland

288 *Incomplete*

What moves men of genius, or rather what inspires their work, is not new ideas, but their obsession with the idea that what has already been said is still not enough.

Eugene Delacroix (1798–1863), France

Music

289 *Flight of sound*

Music is a moral law. It gives soul to the universe, wings to the mind, flight to the imagination and charm and gaiety to life and to everything.

Plato (c.429–c.347BCE), Greece

290 *Above all*

I despise a world which does not feel that music is a higher revelation than all wisdom and philosophy.

Ludwig van Beethoven (1770–1827), Germany/Austria

291 Central essence

All deep things are Song.
It seems somehow the very central
essence of us ... as if all the rest were
but wrappages and hulls!

Thomas Carlyle (1795–1881), Scotland/England

292 *Play on*

Love cannot express the idea
of music, while music may give
an idea of love.

Louis-Hector Berlioz (1803–1869), France

293 Good vibrations

Music and rhythm find their way into the secret places of the soul.

Plato (c.429–c.347BCE), Greece

294 Satisfaction

Music produces a kind of pleasure which human nature cannot do without.

Confucius (551–479BCE), China

295 Two-way traffic

Music is God's gift to man, the only art of Heaven given to earth, the only art of earth we take to Heaven.

Walter Savage Landor (1775–1864), England/Italy

296 Dim secrets

Music takes us out of the actual and whispers to us dim secrets that startle our wonder as to who we are, and for what, whence, and whereto.

Ralph Waldo Emerson (1803–1882), USA

Literature

297 Life-blood

A good book is the precious life-blood of a master spirit,
embalmed and treasured up on a purpose to a life beyond life.

John Milton (1608–1674), England

298 Manifold meanings

A book is a garden, an orchard, a storehouse, a party,
a company by the way, a counsellor, a multitude of counsellors.

Henry Ward Beecher (1813–1887), USA

299 Omnipresent

The author, in his work, must be like God in the universe, present everywhere and visible nowhere.

Gustave Flaubert (1821–1880), France

300 Vital pages

Literature is the thought of thinking Souls.

Thomas Carlyle (1795–1881), Scotland/England

301 Shadows

A library is but the soul's burial-ground. It is the land of shadows.

Henry Ward Beecher (1813–1887), USA

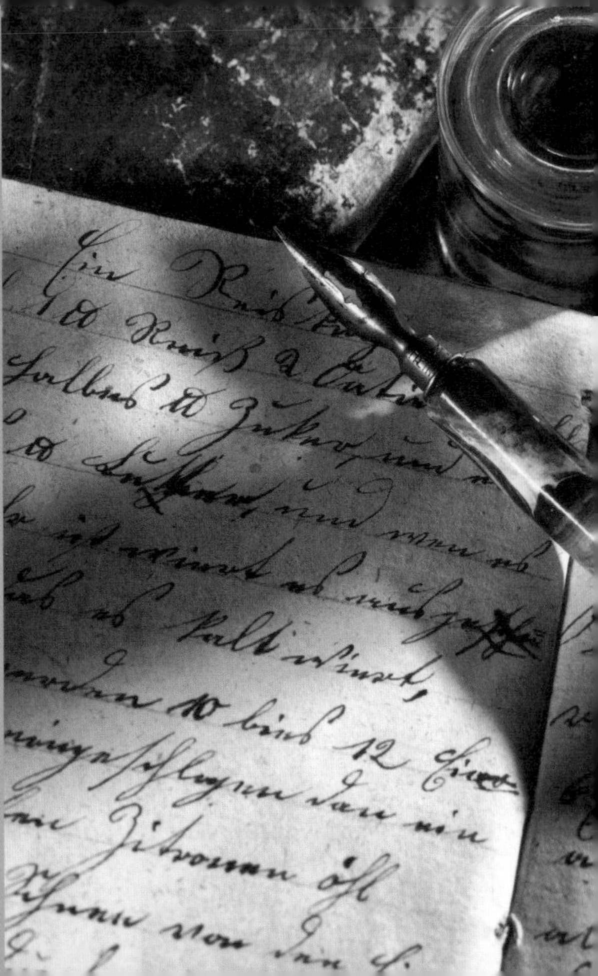

302 Ink plus thought

A small drop of ink
Falling like dew upon a thought, produces
That which makes thousands, perhaps millions think.

Lord Byron (1788–1824), England

303 Fertile crescent

Literature adds to reality, it does not simply describe it.
It enriches the necessary competencies that daily life
requires and provides; and in this respect, it irrigates
the deserts that our lives have already become.

Eduardo Cuadra (1820–1903), Chile

304 Everlasting words

Literature is the immortality of speech.

August Wilhelm von Schlegel (1767–1845), Germany

305 Sublime messages

I decided that it was not wisdom that
enabled poets to write their poetry, but a
kind of instinct or inspiration, such as you
find in seers and prophets who deliver all
their sublime messages without knowing
in the least what they mean.

Socrates (469–399 BCE), Greece

306 Arctic escape

A book must be an ice-axe to break the seas frozen inside our soul.

Franz Kafka (1883–1924), Austria

307 Health check

The decline of literature indicates the decline of a nation.

Johann Wolfgang von Goethe (1749–1832), Germany

Architecture
and design

308 *Noble art*

Architecture aims at Eternity.

*Christopher Wren (1632–1723),
England*

309 Quick, a pencil!

I prefer drawing to talking. Drawing is faster,
and leaves less room for lies.

Le Corbusier (1887–1965), France/Switzerland

310 Three conditions

The end is to build well.
Well building hath three conditions:
      firmness, commodity and delight.

Sir Henry Wotton (1568–1639), England, after Vitruvius,
a Roman architect

311 Finding design

Design in art is a recognition of the relation between various things, various elements in the creative flux. You can't invent a design. You recognize it, in the fourth dimension. That is, with your blood and your bones, as well as with your eyes.

D.H. Lawrence (1885–1930), England

312 Divine offspring

Light, God's eldest daughter, is a principal beauty in a building.

Thomas Fuller (1608–1661), England

313 *Under the sky*

Buildings, too, are children of Earth and Sun.

Frank Lloyd Wright (1867–1959), USA

314 Spirit of the age

Architecture is the will of an epoch translated into space.

Ludwig Mies van der Rohe (1886–1969), Germany

315 Artificial

A structure becomes architectural, and not sculptural, when its elements no longer have their justification in nature.

Guillaume Apollinaire (1880–1918), Italy/France

316 Let it be

When your work speaks for itself, don't interrupt.

Henry John Kaiser (1882–1967), USA

Truth and insight

317 *Right there*

If you cannot find the truth right where you are, where else do you expect to find it? Dogen belief consists in accepting the affirmations of the soul; unbelief, denying them.

Ralph Waldo Emerson (1803–1882), USA

318 *Over and above*

The personal life deeply lived always expands into truths beyond itself.

Anaïs Nin (1903–1977), France

319 *Penmanship*

The ink of the scholar is more sacred than the blood of the martyr.

Prophet Muhammad (c.570–632), Saudi Arabia

320 *Gleaming fire*

True form is magnificently illuminated with gleaming fire.
True wisdom is total silence amid the ringing of wind chimes.

Hongzhi Zhengjue (1091–1157), China

321 *Lovely residue*

The pain passes, but the beauty remains.

Pierre Auguste Renoir (1841–1919), France

322 The mind's burden

Human reason has this peculiar fate that in one species of its knowledge it is burdened by questions which, as prescribed by the very nature of reason itself, it is not able to ignore, but which, as transcending all its powers, it is also not able to answer.

Immanuel Kant (1724–1804), Germany

323 True self

It is not the body, nor the personality, that is the true self. The true self is eternal. Even on the point of death we can say to ourselves, "My true self is free. I cannot be contained."

Marcus Aurelius (121–180), Rome

324 *Under your nose*

You wander from room to room
hunting for the diamond necklace
that is already around your neck!

Jalil al-Din Rumi (1207–1273), Persia

325 Detective work

All truths are easy to understand once they
are discovered: the point is to discover them.

Galileo Galilei (1564–1642), Italy

326 Delving deeper

A little philosophy inclineth man's mind to atheism,
but depth in philosophy bringeth men's minds about
to religion.

Francis Bacon (1561–1626), England

The beauty of numbers

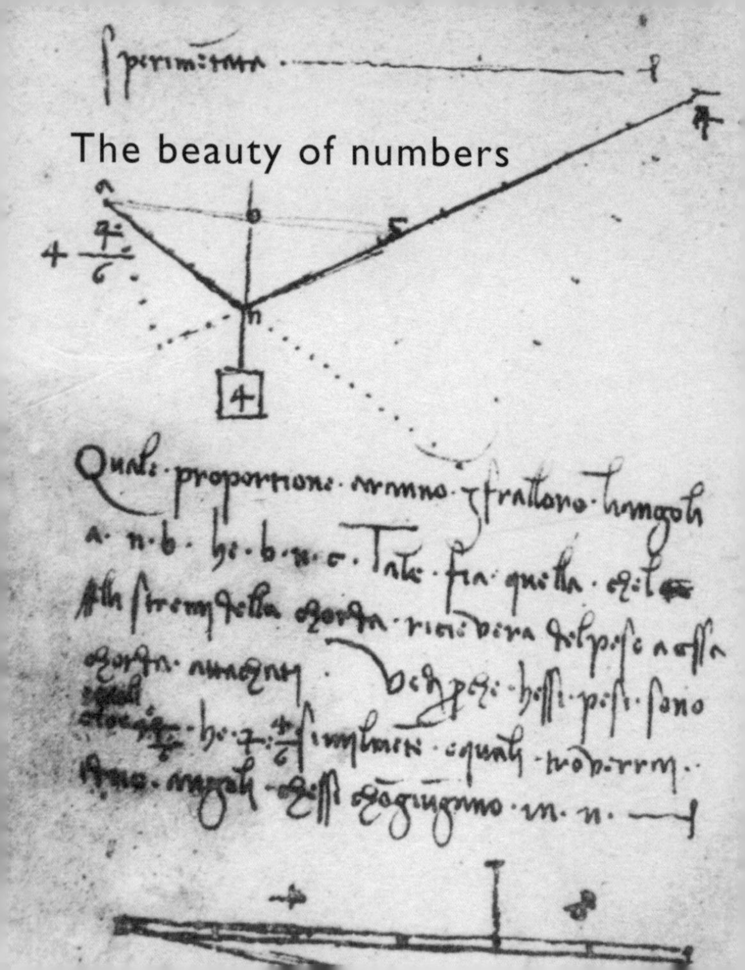

327 Shapeshifter

Geometry enlightens the intellect and sets one's mind right. All of its proofs are very clear and orderly. It is hardly possible for errors to enter into geometrical reasoning, because it is well arranged and orderly. Thus, the mind that constantly applies itself to geometry is not likely to fall into error. In this convenient way, the person who knows geometry acquires intelligence.

Ibn Khaldun (1332–1406), Tunisia

328 Watchful ones

Numbers are intellectual witnesses that belong only to mankind.

Honoré de Balzac (1799–1850), France

329 Ice queen

Mathematics, rightly viewed, possesses not only truth, but supreme beauty – a beauty cold and austere, like that of sculpture.

Bertrand Russell (1872–1970), England/USA

330 Soulful work

It is impossible to be a mathematician without being a poet in one's soul.

Sofia Kovalevskaya (1850–1891), Russia

331 Calculus

God does arithmetic.

Carl Friedrich Gauss (1777–1855), Germany

The spiritual dimension

The sublime

Colour and light

The soul's beauty

Nature's wisdom

The sublime

332 *Mind's abyss*

The mind feels itself set in motion in representation of the sublime in nature; this movement, especially in its inception, may be compared with a vibration with a rapidly alternating repulsion and attraction produced by one and the same object. The point of excess for the imagination is like an abyss in which it fears to lose itself.

Immanuel Kant (1724–1804), Germany

333 *Selflessness*

The most sublime act is to set another before you.

William Blake (1757–1827), England

334 *Fine distinctions*

That we may examine picturesque objects with more ease, it may be
useful to class them into the sublime, and the beautiful; though, in
fact, this distinction is rather inaccurate. Sublimity alone cannot make
an object picturesque. However grand the mountain or the rock may
be, it has no claim to this epithet, unless its form, its colour, or its
accompaniments have some degree of beauty. Nothing can be more
sublime than the ocean: but wholly unaccompanied, it has little
of the picturesque.

William Gilpin (1724–1804), England

335 *Awesome*

There is a sacred horror about everything grand. It is easy to admire mediocrity and hills; but whatever is too lofty, a genius as well as a mountain, an assembly as well as a masterpiece, seen too near, is appalling.

Victor Hugo (1802–1885), France

336 Desert grandeur

The glories and the beauties of form, color, and sound unite in the Grand Canyon – forms unrivalled even by the mountains, colors that vie with sunsets, and sounds that span the diapason from tempest to tinkling raindrop, from cataract to bubbling fountain.

John Wesley Powell (1834–1902), USA

Giant's causeway

The noise resembles the roar of heavy, distant surf. Standing on the stirring ice one can imagine it is disturbed by the breathing and tossing of a mighty giant below.

Ernest Shackleton (1874–1922), England/Ireland

Colour and light

338 *Apples and oranges*

Colour is the fruit of life.

Guillaume Apollinaire (1880–1918), Italy/France

339 *Free thinking*

Colour ... thinks by itself, independently of the object it clothes.

Charles Baudelaire (1821–1867), France/Belgium

340 *Looking up*

Turn your face to the sun and
the shadows fall behind you.

Maori proverb

341 *Monochrome*

Moonlight is sculpture.

Nathaniel Hawthorne (1804–1864), USA

342 *Light and dark*

And the light shineth in darkness; and
the darkness comprehended it not.

John 1:5

343 *Prime hue*

Green is the prime colour of the world and that from which its loveliness arises.

Pedro Calderón de la Barca (1600–1681), Spain

344 *Heavenly*

Blue colour is everlastingly appointed by the Deity to be a source of delight.

John Ruskin (1819–1900), England

345 Pure expression

Mere colour, unspoiled by meaning and unallied with
definite form, can speak to the soul in a thousand
different ways.

Oscar Wilde (1854–1900), England

346 Epiphany

Light is not so much something that reveals,
as it is itself the revelation.

James Turrell (b.1943), USA

The soul's beauty

347 Being prepared

The soul should always stand ajar.
That if the heaven inquire,
He will not be obliged to wait,
Or shy of troubling her.

Emily Dickinson (1830–1886), USA

348 Optional extra

All men's souls are immortal, but the souls
of the righteous are immortal and divine.

Socrates (469–399 BCE), Greece

349 Sea, sky and soul

There is a great spectacle, and that is the sea. There is a greater spectacle than the sea, and that is the sky. There is yet a greater spectacle than the sky, and that is the interior of the soul.

Victor Hugo (1802–1885), France

350 By appointment

Beauty has been appointed by the Deity to be one of the elements by which the human soul is continually sustained; it is therefore to be found more or less in all natural objects.

John Ruskin (1819–1900), England

351 *Two sweet friends*

There are two birds, two sweet friends, who dwell on the self-same tree. The one eats the fruits thereof, and the other looks on in silence.

The first is the human soul who, resting on that tree, though active, feels sad in his unwisdom. But on beholding the power and glory of the higher Spirit, he becomes free from sorrow.

From the Svetasvatara Upanishad *(c.8th century* BCE*), India*

352 *Socratic prayer*

I pray thee, O God, that I may be beautiful within.

Socrates (469–399 BCE), Greece

353 *Baggage*

Though we travel the world over to find the beautiful, we must carry it with us, or we find it not.

Ralph Waldo Emerson (1803–1882), USA

354 Solomon's mercy

Your own soul is nourished when you are kind; it is destroyed when you are cruel.

King Solomon (848–796BCE), Israel

Nature's wisdom

355 Natural eloquence

And this, our life, exempt from public haunt,
Finds tongues in trees, books in the running brooks,
Sermons in stones, and good in everything.

William Shakespeare (1564–1616), from As You Like It, *England*

356 No pulpit

Nature teaches more than she preaches. There are no
sermons in stones. It is easier to get a spark out of a
stone than a moral.

John Burroughs (1837–1921), USA

357 *Woodwork*

What I know of the divine sciences and Holy Scripture,
I learned in woods and fields. I have had no other
masters than the beeches and the oaks.

St Bernard of Clairvaux (1091–1153), France

358 *Concordance*

Never does nature say one thing and wisdom another.

Juvenal (late 1st/early 2nd century), Rome

359 Spring blossom

Petals of the peach blossom
unfolding in the spring breeze,
sweeping aside all doubts
amid the distractions of
leaves and branches.

Dogen (1200–1253), Japan

360 Now is the time

On a cosmic scale, our life is insignificant, yet this brief
period when we appear in the world is the time in which
all meaningful questions arise.

Paul Ricœur (1913–2005), France

361 *All for the best*

The inscrutable wisdom through which we exist is not
less worthy of veneration in respect to what it denies
us than in respect to what it has granted.

Immanuel Kant (1724–1804), Germany

362 *Folds of faith*

Nature's so-called laws are the waving of God's garments,
waving so because he is thinking and loving and walking
inside them.

George Macdonald (1824–1905), Scotland

363 The fullness of time

Anything that falls in the snow comes to light in the thaw.

Danish proverb

364 Music lesson

The brook would lose its song if you took away the rocks.

American proverb

365 Mutual assistance

Be like the mouth and the hand. When the hand is hurt, the mouth blows on it. When the mouth is hurt, the hand rubs it.

African proverb

Index of first lines

T

Index of authors and sources

Acknowledgments

Acknowledgments have been listed by quotation number.

12 from PARACRITICISMS: SEVEN SPECULATIONS OF THE TIMES by Ihab Hassan (University of Illinois Press, 1985). Copyright © Ihab Hassan. Reprinted by permission.

14 "The World" from THE COLLECTED POEMS OF KATHLEEN RAINE, Golgonooza Press, Ipswitch, 2000. Copyright © Kathleen Raine 2000. Reprinted by permission of Golgonooza (UK) and Counterpoint Press (US), a member of Perseus Books Group;

18 "In No Way" by David Ignatow from NEW AND COLLECTED POEMS 1970–1985 (Wesleyan University Press, 1986). Copyright © 1986 by David Ignatow and reprinted by permission of Wesleyan University Press;

19 from THE LITTLE PRINCE by Antoine de Saint-Exupéry (Harvest Books, 2000). Reprinted by permission of Harcourt, Inc;

21, 116, 200, 237, 269, 303 translations copyright © Duncan Baird Publishers, London 2007;

24 "April Rain Song", from THE COLLECTED POEMS OF LANGSTON HUGHES by Langston Hughes, edited by Arnold Rampersad with David Roessel, Associate Editor, copyright © 1994 by The Estate of Langston Hughes. Used by permission of Alfred A. Knopf, a division of Random House, Inc., and David Higham Associates Ltd.;

30, 246, 347 from THE POEMS OF EMILY DICKINSON: READING EDITION edited by Ralph W. Franklin, Cambridge, Mass.: The Belknap Press of Harvard University Press, Copyright © 1998, 1999 by the President and Fellows of Harvard College. Copyright © 1951, 1955, 1979, 1983 by the President and Fellows of Harvard College. Reprinted by permission of the publishers, and the Trustees of Amherst College;

31 from MAD IN PURSUIT by Violette Leduc (Farrar, Straus & Giroux, 1971). Reprinted by permission of the publishers;

35 "The Botticellian Trees" (excerpt) by

William Carlos Williams, from THE COLLECTED POEMS OF WILLIAM CARLOS WILLIAMS: 1909–1939, VOLUME I, copyright © 1965 by Denise Levertov. Reprinted by permission of New Directions Publishing Corp., New York, and Carcanet Press Ltd, Manchester;

41, 158, 217 copyright © DBP;

55 by Albert Einstein, from an interview in the New York Times, 25 April 1929. Reprinted with permission of The Albert Einstein Archives of the Hebrew University of Jerusalem;

65 from THE SACRED PIPE: BLACK ELK'S ACCOUNT OF THE SEVEN RITES OF THE OGLALA SIOUX by Black Elk, recorded and edited by Joseph Epes Brown (University of Oklahoma Press, 1953). Copyright © University of Oklahoma Press. Reprinted by permission of the publishers;

68 from THE SENSE OF WONDER by Rachel Carson. Copyright © 1956 by Rachel L. Carson. Reprinted by permission of Frances Collin, Trustee;

89 attributed to Archibald MacLeish, precise source unknown, extract from his unpublished manuscripts now in the public domain;

102 from "Brother Body" in POINTING THE WAY, COLLECTED ESSAYS by Martin Buber (Harper, 1957). Translation copyright © Maurice Friedman. Reprinted by permission of The Balkin Agency, Inc., as the literary representative of The Estate of Martin Buber;

105 from "I am a Dancer", a statement by Martha Graham. Copyright © 2000–2006, Martha Graham Center of Contemporary Dance. All rights reserved;

114 from THE DIARY OF A YOUNG GIRL: THE DEFINITIVE EDITION by Anne Frank, edited by Otto H. Frank and Mirjam Pressler, translated by Susan Massotty (Viking, 1997), copyright © The Anne Frank-Fonds, Basle, Switzerland, 1991. English translation copyright © Doubleday, a division of Bantam Doubleday Dell Publishing Group, Inc., 1995. Reproduced by permission of Penguin Books Ltd., and Doubleday, a division of Random House, Inc.;

121 from THE HOUSE OF EUROPE by Paul Scott Mowrer (Boston: Houghton Mifflin, 1945). Reprinted by permission of the publishers;

124 from PRINCIPLES OF SOCIAL

RECONSTRUCTION by Bertrand Russell (Routledge, 2005). Copyright © 1927, 2005. Reproduced by permission of Taylor & Francis Books UK, and The Bertrand Russell Peace Foundation Ltd.;

132, 222, 261 from A SAND COUNTY ALMANAC AND SKETCHES HERE AND THERE (OUTDOOR ESSAYS & REFLECTIONS) by Leopold, Aldo (Oxford University Press, USA, 1992). Used by permission of Oxford University Press, Inc.;

133 attributed to M.K. Gandhi, precise source unknown. Reprinted by permission of the Navajivan Trust (Estate of Mohandas K. Gandhi);

150 from DANG DANG DOKO DANG by Osho. Copyright © 1977 by Osho International Foundation, Switzerland (www.osho.com). All rights reserved. Reprinted with permission;

161 attributed to Rabindranath Tagore, precise source unknown. Reprinted by permission of Visva-Bharati University;

162 from THE ART OF PEACE by Morihei Ueshiba, translated and edited by John Stevens © 2002. Used by arrangement with Shambhala Publications Ltd., Boston, MA, www.shambhala.com;

183 from THE SEA AROUND US by Rachel Carson. Copyright © 1950 by Rachel L. Carson. Used by permission of Frances Collin, Trustee;

187 from FIFTEEN YEARS OF MARTIN BUXBAUM'S TABLE TALK by Martin Buxbaum (Popular Library, 1972). Reprinted by permission of Hachette Book Group, USA;

193 from SIDDHARTHA by Hermann Hesse (Picador, 1998). Reprinted by permission of Peter Owen Ltd., as the literary representative of The Estate of Hermann Hesse;

197 by Thor Heyerdahl, quoted in THOR HEYERDAHL, THE EXPLORER by Snorre Evensberget (Oslo: J.M. Sternersens Forlag A.S., 1994). Copyright © Thor Heyerdahl. Reprinted by permission of The Estate of Thor Heyerdahl;

206 from REMEMBRANCE ROCK, Volume 1, by Carl Sandburg copyright 1948 by Harcourt, Inc., and renewed 1976 by Lilian Steichen Sandburg, Margaret Sandburg, Janet Sandburg, and Helga Sandburg, reprinted by permission of the publisher;

228 from an Address given by President Eisenhower at Bradley University, Peoria,

Illinois, September 25, 1956. Used by permission of John S.D. Eisenhower (the Estate of Dwight David Eisenhower);

253 spoken by Sir Edmund Hillary. Used by permission of Celebrity Speakers (NZ) Ltd., as the literary representative of The Estate of Sir Edmund Hillary;

254 from THE PRACTICE OF THE WILD by Gary Snyder (North Point Press, 1990). Reprinted by permission of Farrar, Straus & Giroux, New York;

259 from ADVENTURES OF IDEAS by Alfred North Whitehead. Copyright © 1933 by the Macmillan Company; copyright renewed © 1961 by Evelyn Whitehead. Reprinted with the permission of Cambridge University Press, and Scribner, an imprint of Simon and Schuster Adult Publishing Group. All rights reserved;

266 from THE PERENNIAL PHILOSOPHY by Aldous Huxley. Copyright © 1944, 1945 by Aldous Huxley. Copyright renewed 1973, 1974 by Laura A. Huxley. Reprinted by permission of HarperCollins Publishers, and The Reece Halsey Agency as the literary representative of The Estate of Aldous Huxley;

268 from GEOGRAPHY, RESOURCES, AND ENVIRONMENT: SELECTED WRITINGS OF GILBERT F. WHITE, VOLUME I by Gilbert F. White, edited by Robert W. Kates and Ian Burton (University of Chicago Press, 1975). Copyright © 1986 by The University of Chicago. All rights reserved. Reprinted by permission of the publishers;

285 from "Solitude" by Magdalena Abakanowicz taken from THEORIES AND DOCUMENTS OF CONTEMPORARY ART: A SOURCEBOOK OF ARTISTS' WRITINGS by Peter Selz and Kristine Stiles (University of California Press, 1995). Copyright © Magdalena Abakanowicz, courtesy, Malborough Gallery, New York. Reprinted by permission;

287 from MODERN MAN IN SEARCH OF A SOUL by Carl Jung (Routledge and Kegan Paul, 1962). Copyright © Carl Jung. Reproduced by permission of Taylor & Francis Books UK;

309 spoken by Le Corbusier, from an article entitled "Corbu" in Time Magazine 5 May 1961. Copyright © FLC/DACS, 2007. Used by permission of Le Corbusier Foundation;

314 from MIES RECONSIDERED: HIS

CAREER, LEGACY, AND DISCIPLES, organized by John Zukowsky (Rizzoli, 1986). Used with permission from Rizzoli International Publications, Inc.;

318 from THE DIARY OF ANAÏS NIN, VOLUME TWO (1934–1939) by Anaïs Nin (Swallow Press, 1967). Copyright © 1967, 1970 by Anaïs Nin. All rights reserved. Reprinted by permission of the Author's Representative, Barbara W. Stuhlmann, and the publishers;

329 from MYSTICISM AND LOGIC by Bertrand Russell (Longmans, Green & Co., 1918). Reproduced by permission of The Bertrand Russell Peace Foundation Ltd.;

360 from TIME AND NARRATIVE, VOLUME I by Paul Ricœur, translated by Kathleen McLaughlin and David Pellauer (University of Chicago Press, 1990). Originally published as TEMPS ET RECIT © Editions du Seuil, 1983. Copyright © 1984 by The University of Chicago. All rights reserved. Reprinted by permission of the publishers.

The publishers have made every effort to trace copyright holders, but if anyone has been omitted we apologize and will, if informed, make corrections in any future edition.

Photographic credits

The publisher would like to thank the following people and photographic libraries for permission to reproduce their material. Every care has been taken to trace copyright holders. However, if we have omitted anyone we apologize and will, if informed, make corrections in future printings.

Page: 2 Sebun Photos/Getty Images; **5** Dave Tully/Flowerphotos.com; **6-7** Craig Tuttle/Corbis; **8-9** Theo Allofs/Getty; **11** Roger Ressmeyer/Corbis; **14-15** Frank Krahmer/Corbis; **19** Taxi Getty; **20-21** Whit Preston/Getty; **24-25** Patrick Bennett/Corbis; **28-29** Charlie Waite/Getty; **32-33** Lee Foster/Getty; **39** Theo Allofs/Getty; **40-41** Frank Lukasseck/Corbis; **44-45** Jim Craigmyle/Corbis; **50-51** William Manning/Corbis; **54-55** Joe McDonald/Corbis; **60-61** Adam Jones/Oxford Scientific Library/Photo Library; **66-67** Michael S Quinton/Getty; **72-73** Marianne Majerus Photography; **76-77** Douglas Peebles/Corbis; **78-79** Orion Press/Getty; **82-83** Arthur Morris/Corbis; **86-87** Philip James Corwin/Corbis; **88-89** Ferdinando Scianna/Magnum Photos; **92** Dennis Cooper/Corbis; **98-99** Paul A. Souder/Corbis; **104-105** Veer Daniel H Bailey/Getty; **108-109** Renee Lynn/Corbis; **113** Angel Medina/Corbis; **116-117** Joaquin Palting/Corbis; **119** Ferdinando Scianna/Magnum; **123** Paul Edmondson/Getty; **124-125** Victoria Gomez/Flowerphotos.com; **126-127** Eddie Judd/Flowerphotos.com; **130-131** Peter Straw/Flowerphotos.com; **132-133** Hiroji Kubota/Magnum Photos; **138-139** Michelle Garrett/Corbis; **141** Craig Tuttle/Corbis; **144-145** Martin Harvey/NHPA; **148** Frans Lemmens/Corbis; **150-151** Britta Jaschinski; **152-153** Paul A.Stouders/Corbis; **154** Shannon Fagan/Getty; **159** Beverly Joubert/Getty; **165** Peter Straw/Flowerphotos.com; **168-169** Marianne Majerus Photography; **170-171** Sue Bishop/Flowersphotos.com; **175** Grant